Adria Kennedy is a 25-year-old travelling missionary who enjoys painting, drawing, writing poetry, music, and discussing important topics. She has been interested in various forms of art from a very young age. Adria has won several writing and visual arts awards throughout elementary school and high school, including winning the art award at her high school graduation.

Adria wrote *Trapped Inside a Tragedy* when she was 20 years old, and then endeavoured to illustrate and publish it.

To see more of the author's work, find her on Instagram @_paint_and_poetry_

# TRAPPED INSIDE
# A TRAGEDY

ADRIA KENNEDY

## AUSTIN MACAULEY PUBLISHERS™
LONDON • CAMBRIDGE • NEW YORK • SHARJAH

A CIP catalogue record for this title is available from the British Library.

ISBN 9781035829118 (Paperback)
ISBN 9781035829125 (Hardback)
ISBN 9781035829132 (ePub e-book)

www.austinmacauley.com

First Published 2024
Austin Macauley Publishers Ltd®
1 Canada Square
Canary Wharf
London
E14 5AA

To my family, who has always accepted my authentic self.

I am eternally grateful for my mum and dad, who have always encouraged my creativity, inspired me to work hard, and made me feel seen.

As well, I would like to thank Austin Macauley Publishers for turning this dream into a reality.

# The Show: A Tragedy

Oh us? We live in luxury,
With much more than we need.
We must fulfill our fantasy,
Of power, wealth, and greed.

We act it out quite perfectly-
The roles of king and queen-

But our lower-class reality,
Remains behind the scenes.

Yes, though we look like royalty,
We are not what we seem.
We're secretly in misery,
Just faking self-esteem.

We try to find security
In superficial means;
We place ourselves on hierarchies
To make sure we are seen.

The crowd is our affinity;
We live to see them pleased,

But in our dreaded privacy,
We do not feel at ease.

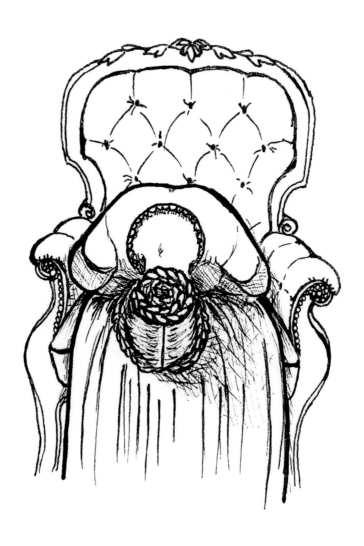

It's in our genealogy;
It's in our DNA:
A long-lived, broken legacy
Of tension in our veins.
The pattern in our ancestry
Has never changed with age:
We long for authenticity,
Yet crave the dazzling stage.
We feel it is our destiny
To keep our blood this way,
For, though it screams calamity,
It's in our family name.

It gives us an identity,
Though somber and mundane.
The mask and costume novelty
Preserves our precious fame.

Besides, it comes so naturally-
The characters we play-
We know the script instinctively;
We're *born* to entertain.

And though we are in agony,
We do not try to change,
For, as we know, a tragedy
Must end in utter pain.

# Marjorie's Soliloquy

Wake up! We're living foolishly!
Just listen to yourselves:
Your words are contradictory;
You're calling sickness, "health!"

We're living in idolatry;
The crowd consumes our thoughts.
And what defines our victory?
The size of the applause?!

We follow suit robotically:
The script decides our life.
See, now it's my soliloquy.
How long will I comply?

I must not choose conformity,
Not for a single scene.
I will not let my family
Decide who I must be.

**Marjorie**  Oh listen to me, family,
I've wisdom I must share!
I've captured an epiphany,
And hide it I don't dare:

We're more than just a drama team,
We're more than what we own.
Let's drop the vain conspiracy
That life is just a show!

| | |
|---|---|
| **Uncle Ernest** | You kid yourself, Miss Marjorie!<br>We're *here* to entertain.<br>If we don't please society,<br>We're worthless and disdained. |
| **Marjorie** | You think that popularity<br>Defines what you are worth?<br>You've sold yourselves to slavery,<br>Denying that you're hurt. |

| **Aunt Guinevere** | We are not hurt, Dear Marjorie,<br>If we enjoy the pain<br>I'll walk through flames and rampancy<br>To save the family name. |
|---|---|
| **Marjorie** | You've mixed up your priorities;<br>Your health is what comes first.<br>Forget the fame and luxury,<br>It will not quench your thirst!<br><br>I will resist society.<br>I've fallen from the tree.<br>I've realized my identity<br>Is more than just my genes. |

| | |
|---|---|
| **Mother**<br>**Marigold** | My love, you've lost your sanity,<br>We need you on our team.<br>Oh look, put on this jewellery,<br>You'll make a perfect queen. |
| **Marjorie** | How dare you try to limit me<br>To costumes, masks, and moulds?<br>I *will* not be your strategy<br>For reaching empty goals. |
| | Don't use me for your puppetry,<br>My life is not a show.<br>I will not join your industry<br>To build your kingdom throne. |

**Cousin**
**Elizabeth**   I think you've lost your memory!
Forget not what we've done:
We saved you from great poverty
By making you someone.

**Sister**
**Agatha**   *Indeed* you've lost your memory!
Forget not where you're from–
A line of Broadway prodigies;
Without us, you're *no-one.*

**Marjorie**    Your ignorance is killing me-
Alas! Is this a joke?
Go find some rationality,
I've *had* it with you folk!

*Soliloquy*    I've tried to help my family,
They won't give up their ways.
It's time to leave this tragedy,
My comedy awaits.

# Extra

# More

Costumes, makeup, jewellery,
Ruffles, frills, and lace,
Pearls, wigs, masks, such gluttony!
Oh bring it all with haste!

More and more for fallacy;
Do cover all my flaws.
Yes, they shall see supremacy!
So bow down! Drop your jaw!

# Rain

Our anguish is like pouring rain,
A mask is our umbrella.
But should there come a hurricane,
Concealment's our dilemma.
See though we've means to veil the face,
We cannot hide forever.
The mask comes off, the music fades,
And thus, so must the pleasure.
You'll find it odd- perhaps insane-
The rashness of our measures,
To cover up our ugly pain
Instead of bear the weather.
But though we walk through blazing flames
To maintain our endeavour,
The people think our selfish aim
Is of a good-will effort.
We must maintain our picture frame;
Illusion's our protector.
For if we're caught, we'll be disdained;
We'll lose our fame and treasure.

# Oblivion

We strut and stride so aimlessly;
Ignoring what is real.
Our fame and wealth too primary
To give up our ideals.

A blindfold for oblivion,
A mask to hide the pain.
A costume for illusion n'
A show for selfish gain.

# Golden Crate

You're stuck inside a golden crate,
And yet you hold the key.

You've every means to thus escape,
But gold sways, "no don't leave."

# Conclusion

There's no such thing as liberty.
There's no way to live happily.
So we'll embrace captivity,
Trapped inside our tragedy.

# The Poem in its
# Original Format

# The Show: A Tragedy

Oh us? We live in luxury,
With much more than we need.
We must fulfill our fantasy
Of power, wealth, and greed.
We act it out quite perfectly-
The roles of king and queen-
But our lower-class reality
Remains behind the scenes.
Yes, though we look like royalty,
We are not what we seem.
We're secretly in misery,
Just faking self-esteem.
We try to find security
In superficial means;
We place ourselves on hierarchies
To make sure we are seen.
The crowd is our affinity;
We live to see them pleased,
But in our dreaded privacy,
We do not feel at ease.

It's in our genealogy;
It's in our DNA:
A long-lived, broken legacy
Of tension in our veins.
The pattern in our ancestry

Has never changed with age:
We long for authenticity,
Yet crave the dazzling stage.
We feel it is our destiny
To keep our blood this way,
For, though it screams calamity,
It's in our family name.
It gives us an identity,
Though somber and mundane.
The mask and costume novelty
Preserves our precious fame.
Besides, it comes so naturally-
The characters we play-
We know the script instinctively;
We're *born* to entertain.

And though we are in agony,
We do not try to change,
For, as we know, a tragedy
Must end in utter pain.

**Marjorie's Soliloquy**

Wake up! We're living foolishly!
Just listen to yourselves:
Your words are contradictory;
You're calling sickness, "health!"

We're living in idolatry;
The crowd consumes our thoughts.

And what defines our victory?
The size of the applause?!

We follow suit robotically:
The script decides our life.
See, now it's my soliloquy.
How long will I comply?

I must not choose conformity,
Not for a single scene.
I will not let my family
Decide who I must be.

## The Stubborn, Helpless Family

**Marjorie**    Oh listen to me, family,
I've wisdom I must share!
I've captured an epiphany,
And hide it I don't dare:

We're more than just a drama team,
We're more than what we own.
Let's drop the vain conspiracy
That life is just a show!

**Uncle**    You kid yourself, Miss Marjorie!
**Ernest**    We're here to entertain.
If we don't please society,
We're worthless and disdained.

**Marjorie**   You think that popularity
Defines what you are worth?
You've sold yourselves to slavery,
Denying that you're hurt.

**Aunt**   We are not hurt, Dear Marjorie,
**Guinevere**   If we enjoy the pain.
I'll walk through flames and rampancy
To save the family name.

**Marjorie**   You've mixed up your priorities;
Your health is what comes first.
Forget the fame and luxury,
It will not quench your thirst!

I will resist society.
I've fallen from the tree.
I've realized my identity
Is more than just my genes.

**Mother**   My love, you've lost your sanity,
**Marigold**   We need you on our team.
Oh look, put on this jewellery,
You'll make a perfect queen.

**Marjorie**   How dare you try to limit me
To costumes, masks, and moulds?
I will not be your strategy
For reaching empty goals.

Don't use me for your puppetry,
My life is not a show.
I will not join your industry
To build your kingdom throne.

**Cousin**
**Elizabeth**
I think you've lost your memory!
Forget not what we've done:
We saved you from great poverty
By making you someone.

**Sister**
**Agatha**
*Indeed* you've lost your memory!
Forget not where you're from-
A line of Broadway prodigies;
Without us, you're no-one.

**Marjorie**
Your ignorance is killing me-
Alas! Is this a joke?
Go find some rationality,
I've had it with you folk!

*Soliloquy*
I've tried to help my family,
They won't give up their ways.
It's time to leave this tragedy,
My comedy awaits.

## Extra

### Golden Crate

You're stuck inside a golden crate,
And yet you hold the key.

You've every means to thus escape,
But gold sways, "no don't leave."

### More

Costumes, makeup, jewellery,
Ruffles, frills, and lace,
Pearls, wigs, masks, such gluttony!
Oh bring it all with haste!

More and more for fallacy;
*Do* cover all my flaws.
Yes, they shall see supremacy!
So bow down! Drop your jaw!

### Rain

Our anguish is like pouring rain'
A mask is our umbrella.
But should there come a hurricane,
Concealment's our dilemma.
See though we've means to veil the face,
We cannot hide forever.
The mask comes off, the music fades,
And thus, so must the pleasure.
You'll find it odd- perhaps insane-

The rashness of our measures,
To cover up our ugly pain
Instead of bear the weather.
But though we walk through blazing flames
To maintain our endeavour,
The people think our selfish aim
Is of a good-will effort.
We must maintain our picture frame,
Illusion's our protector.
For if we're caught, we'll be disdained;
We'll lose our fame and treasure.

## Oblivion

We strut and stride so aimlessly;
Ignoring what is real.
Our fame and wealth too primary
To give up our ideals.

A blindfold for oblivion,
A mask to hide the pain.
A costume for illusion n'
A show for selfish gain.

## Conclusion

There's no such thing as liberty.
There's no way to live happily.
So we'll embrace captivity,
Trapped inside our tragedy.

*Written and Illustrated by*
*Adria Kennedy*

*The End!*